There was a price circled in red— $1,250,000.

Whoa! Was that one million!?

As in ONE MILLION TWO HUNDRED AND FIFTY THOUSAND!?

I had to sit down.

Then I read the whole entry.

> *Larry the Lizard* No. 1—36 pages, full color. Artist: Bob Elbo, Jr. Only 800 copies of this comic were printed, and a fire at the warehouse destroyed all but ten copies. Since Elbo went on to become the most famous cartoonist of his day, this scarce early title has become one of the most valuable comic books of all time. Mint condition…$1,250,000.

It had to be a misprint. No comic could be worth *that* much.

For Ethan and Adam
— one more for the collection

http://www.randomhouse.com/

Library of Congress Cataloging-in-Publication Data
Schade, Susan.
Ron Rooney and the million-dollar comic / by Susan Schade ;
illustrated by Jon Buller. p. cm. "A Stepping Stone book."
SUMMARY: Comic book fan Ron Rooney tries to trick a fellow collector into selling him
his copy of "Larry the Lizard" issue number one because Ron believes that it will
become rare and valuable in the future.
ISBN: 0-679-87385-6 (trade) — ISBN: 0-679-97385-0 (lib. bdg.) [1. Cartoons
and comics—Collectors and collecting—Fiction.] I. Buller, Jon, ill. II. Title.
PZ7.B9135M1 1996 [Fic]—dc20 95-32721

Printed in the United States of America 10 9 8 7 6 5 4 3 2 1

RON ROONEY AND THE MILLION-DOLLAR COMIC

by Jon Buller
and Susan Schade

A STEPPING STONE BOOK

Random House New York

VOYAGE TO THE INVISIBLE PLANET

It started out like any ordinary Saturday. I went to the comic book store. I go to the comic book store every Saturday.

BONGGggggg. The door chime rang in my ears. I let the door swing shut behind me and went down the stairs. I was inside the Invisible Planet. There were comic books to the left of me and comic books to the right of me. Comic books everywhere! Now I was happy.

I spotted some new Ratman reprints

right away. Aldo had them displayed on the front rack.

And there was a hardcover collection that I had never seen before—*The Complete Incredible Skulk!* Cool!

I took a look at the display case. I was glad to see that my favorite model—the Germinator—was still there.

"Hey, it's Ron Rooney, future famous cartoonist," Aldo said to me. "What's happening, Ron?" Aldo runs the store. He also makes all the models himself. And he orders all the comics. Aldo can get you practically any comic you want.

He dipped a tiny brush into the cap of red paint and scraped it to a point. Then he painted a perfect red vein squiggling across a white eyeball. Aldo is good!

"I got a drawing board for my birthday," I said. "It's white, and you can set

it at an angle, and it has a clip-on full-spectrum light!"

"Cool!" said Aldo. "Pretty soon you'll be drawing stuff for Marble Comics!" Aldo takes an interest in my career plans.

He showed me a box of old horror comics that had just come in. "They're pretty well read," he said. "I don't think you'll find any in mint condition."

I snorted through my nose. I don't care about mint condition. That's for stupid fanboy collectors.

I *read* my comics. And I *don't* store them in plastic bags!

BONGGgggggg. Talk about stupid fanboy collectors. Harold Fishbone, the ultimate fanboy collector, clomped down the stairs in his hard-soled shoes. He was carrying a briefcase and a well-thumbed copy of *Backstreet's Buyers Guide*.

"Stand and deliver," Harold said to Aldo.

"Welcome to Earth," Aldo said back.

"Have you got any new first issues?" Harold asked. Harold collects only issue number one of new titles. It really burns me up.

"Don't you know, Harold," I butted in, "that the first issue isn't always the best?

You should see issue number twenty-four of *Doctor Deranged*. You don't get cut-aways like that in issue number one!"

Harold stared at me and blinked. "But will it ever be worth big money?" he asked seriously. "NO!" he answered his own question.

He whipped open his copy of *Back-street's Buyers Guide*. "Don't you ever look

at *Backstreet's*?" he asked. He flipped through the pages and jabbed his finger at some prices that were circled in red.

"One thousand dollars," he read out loud. "Fifteen hundred dollars. *Eight thousand dollars!* All number ones!"

He looked at me like he was worried about my mental health.

"Phooey," I said. I tried to explain it to him. "Those old comics are only worth so much because nobody used to collect comics back then. So old comics in good condition are scarce.

"But now there are lots of guys collecting number ones. They won't be scarce, so they won't be valuable!"

"They *will* be scarce!" Harold practically shrieked. Then he said more calmly, "And I'll tell you why they'll be scarce. Because most of those other kids will get

tired of collecting. And they'll go away to college or something, and their parents will move and throw out their old junk— including their comics!

"But that will never happen to me, because I'm taking my comics with me— everywhere I go! And some of my number ones will become priceless. And do you know what I'm going to do with them?"

"No, what?"

"I'm going to sell them—and go to HARVARD BUSINESS SCHOOL!"

It's no use trying to talk to true fan-boys.

THE MAN WITH THE COOL SHOES

I left Harold to his number ones and got to work on the box of horror comics. You can learn a lot from some of those old artists.

Harold bought a couple of first issues, a box of protective plastic bags, and some backer boards. I heard the door bong as he went out.

For a while the store was quiet. Aldo was working on his Prawn model. Every once in a while he would whistle a few

notes from the theme to *Moon Wars*.

I had found about twenty old comics that I wanted, and at least two that I couldn't live without, when the door chimes went off again.

BONGGggggggg. A bald guy came into the store. From the back he looked sort of like Harold Fishbone's father, except this guy was wearing a shiny purple suit and a white shirt with big collar points. I happen to know that Mr. Fishbone always wears gray business suits with pin-striped button-down shirts.

"Excuse me." The man leaned close to Aldo and kind of whispered in his ear. "Do you have *Larry the Lizard*, number one?"

"Aha!" I thought. This interested me. I had read *Larry the Lizard* many times. In fact, I had practiced drawing Larry the Lizard until I could draw him pretty well.

Then I had made up some characters of my own—Sally the Salamander and Ned the Newt.

Larry the Lizard was the kind of comic I liked best. It wasn't mainstream. It was weird and different. And it was drawn by a new artist I had never heard of before— Bob Elbo, Jr.

"I'm sorry," Aldo said. "I don't have any more copies of *Larry the Lizard*. I only ordered a couple and they're both gone."

The man groaned and sagged against the counter. "Gone," he moaned. "ALL GONE!" He covered his eyes with the back of his hand and staggered up the stairs.

"Cool shoes," I thought to myself as I watched him climb the stairs. They were black-and-white with pointy toes, and I had never seen anything like them before

in the stores around here.

"Hey, wait!" Aldo picked up a piece of paper from the counter. But the door chime bonged, and the man was gone. "Hey, Ron, would you see if you can catch that guy? He left this by mistake."

"Sure." I grabbed the sheet of paper and ran out. Aldo doesn't get up from his stool much. He's pretty slow-moving. But I'm not. I'm pretty fast. So I expected to catch the guy with the cool shoes right outside the store.

But he wasn't there. I looked up the street. I looked down the street. I looked over at the park across the street. He had vanished into thin air!

SUMMER, 2027!

I looked at the paper to see if it was anything important. It was just a page torn out of *Backstreet's Guide*. There was a price circled in red—$1,250,000.

Whoa! Was that one million!? As in ONE MILLION TWO HUNDRED AND FIFTY THOUSAND!?

I had to sit down. Then I read the whole entry.

Larry the Lizard No. 1—36 pages, full color. Artist: Bob Elbo, Jr. Only 800 copies of this comic were printed, and a fire at the warehouse destroyed all but ten copies. Since Elbo went on to become the most famous cartoonist of his day, this scarce early title has become one of the most valuable comic books of all time. Mint condition... $1,250,000.

It must be a misprint. No comic is worth *that* much. Hey, wait a minute. The whole thing was screwy. You can't say, "Elbo went on to become the most famous cartoonist of his day" when his first comic had just come out!

I looked at the entry again, carefully. That's when I noticed the date printed at the top of the page.

Summer, 2027.

No way! Unless...I gasped! Unless I was holding a page from an incredible book— the book that every collector dreams about —a price guide from the future!

The more I thought about it, the more likely it seemed. That guy must have come here from 2027 in some kind of time machine!

That explained everything! The date. The price. The whole story about Bob Elbo, Jr., becoming the greatest cartoonist of his day. The way the guy vanished into

thin air! He must have zapped himself right back to the future!

If only I had known! I would have talked to him in the Invisible Planet. I would have asked him how he did it. Did he have a magic pillow, like the Meditator? Or a time-displacement helmet, like Thunder Woman? Or could he hot-wire a telephone booth, like Hairdevil?

The shoes! I bet those were time-travel shoes!

You may think I had forgotten all about the million-dollar comic. But you would be wrong.

In the back of my mind, I was thinking about it the whole time. And I was getting *real* excited. Because I—I, Ron Rooney— had one of the only ten *Larry the Lizard* number ones in existence!

I owned a million-dollar comic!

DESTINATION — OUTER SPACE

I started running for home with the page from the future scrunched in my sweaty hand.

While I ran, I was thinking, "Maybe it isn't too wrecked—not mint condition, I know, but maybe it's not exactly torn or anything. I hope, I hope, I hope!"

I started looking for *Larry the Lizard* in my room. The pile of comic books on the floor of the closet. The pile next to my bed. The pile under the bed.

21

I went through every comic in my room. Then I went up to the attic, to the corner by the window where I read sometimes.

This wasn't turning out to be easy. Why shouldn't I be lucky? Why shouldn't the next comic in this pile be...*Larry the Lizard*! Nope. Or the next one...? Nope. Or the next one? Nope.

Nope! Nope! Nope! Looking for something I can't find drives me crazy.

"Ron!" It was my sister, Ruth.

"What?"

"What are you looking for?"

Ruth! Maybe Ruth had it! Sometimes I give her my old comics. "Did I give you my *Larry the Lizard* comic?" I said. "I mean, let you read it?" I didn't want there to be any confusion about who owned it.

"Yeah," Ruth said. "It's one of my favorites. That's why I used it."

"'Used it'?! What do you mean, 'USED IT'?" I had Ruth by the shoulders and I was yelling in her face. She started to look worried.

"Why shouldn't I use it?" she asked, wiggling out of my grasp. "You said I could have it."

I tried to calm down. "What did you use it for, Ruth?" I asked, smiling pleasantly at her.

She didn't buy my pleasant smile. She scurried down the stairs. "I put it in the school capsule for the space probe!" she yelled as she ran to the safety of her room.

Thunk! She slammed the door. *Thunk!* I banged my head against the wall. *Thunk! Thunk! Thunk!*

Gone. *Larry the Lizard*—GONE! In the space probe, on its way to some other galaxy!

One million dollars—gone!

OPERATION FISHBONE

I was down but not defeated.

My copy of *Larry the Lizard* might be on its way out of the solar system, but that left nine others. And I bet I knew where one of those other nine copies was.

I bet it was in Harold Fishbone's collection. In mint condition! And Harold didn't know anything about the page from the *Backstreet's Guide* of Summer, 2027! That page was my secret advantage.

I would have to proceed carefully.

After a lot of thought, I decided to steal Harold's copy. I know stealing is wrong. So I would leave some money for it somewhere in Harold's room. Say, double the cover price. You couldn't call that *stealing,* exactly.

I figured that since he never read his comics, he probably didn't even know which ones he had. So he wouldn't even miss it, right?

I called him up to ask if I could come over and see his collection.

"That would be great!" he said.

Harold lives in a square yellow house with window boxes and lace curtains. Mrs. Fishbone met me at the door with a plate of homemade chocolate-chip cookies. "It's so nice to see you, Ron!" she said. "Can you stay for lunch?"

I told her I had to go home for lunch. I

couldn't see myself plotting to not-exactly-steal Harold's comic while his mother was smiling at me and handing me good things to eat.

I did take six cookies, though. Harold said, "This way to the Casbah..." Whatever that is. I followed him upstairs. He keeps his collection in twelve matching suitcases that he stores on their sides in a big closet.

"Comics should be stored flat," he told me as he pulled out a suitcase and stood it on end.

"Each suitcase is locked and tagged with a number," Harold explained. "The numbers correspond with alphabetical lists that I keep in this three-ring binder."

He unclipped a ring of keys from his belt and showed it to me. "The keys are numbered too," he said.

I had to hand it to Harold. It was a
pretty awesome system. Harold took key
number one and put it in the lock of suitcase number one.

"These are all the comics that I got
during my first six months of collecting,"
he said. "I got money for Christmas, and

my dad said I should invest it wisely."

He turned the key and popped open the case. The comics were revealed, all lined up in a kind of hanging file. "Cool!" I breathed. Harold just smiled and pulled the first comic out gently—still in its plastic bag, of course.

"*Aerobus*, number one," he said. "This isn't the first comic I ever bought, though. That was *Ken and Blimpy*, number one."

Harold looked at his suitcase and frowned. "Do you think it's better to keep them in alphabetical order by title, or in chronological order by age, *or* in chronological order by when I got them?" he asked.

You could tell that was the kind of problem that kept Harold awake at night.

I was starting to like Harold. He was a one-of-a-kind. I told him I couldn't decide which order was best, that I would have to think about it.

Harold had some really good comics. Of course, a few of them were junk. I told him they would never be worth anything.

He didn't pull them out of his collection, but he did make some notes in his

notebooks. "R. R. says worthless," or "Top artist—R. R."

I liked having my comments in Harold's notebooks. "And this is my *Larry the Lizard*, number one," Harold said. My eyes bulged. It was beautiful! MINT!

I was looking at a million-dollar comic!

THE ART OF THE DEAL

My fingers itched to grab the million-dollar comic and run. The heck with Mrs. Fishbone's cookies and Harold's cool suitcases and the little notes about "R.R. says."

I tried to calm down. "Don't do anything stupid," I said to myself. "You have plenty of time. Years, even."

To Harold, I said, "Cool. That's a good comic. You should read it sometime."

He wrote, "Good—R. R." in his notebook. He wanted to show me his coin col-

lection, but I said I had to go. I needed to think. I had decided that even not-exactly-stealing was wrong. Besides, I didn't see how I could get away with it. Not with Harold's fanatic fanboy system.

On the way home, I was thinking that becoming a millionaire is not so easy. I decided to try something else.

When I got home I called Harold on the phone. "Communication system engaged," a voice intoned. "Proceed."

"Huh?" I said.

"Oh, hi, Ron," Harold said.

"It was fun seeing your collection, Harold," I said. "Uh, you have one comic I would really like to have. I wondered if you would sell it to me?"

"Oh." Long pause. I guessed Harold wasn't too eager to part with any of his comics.

"Well," he finally said, "I wasn't really planning on selling any of them yet. Can't you get it from the Invisible Planet?"

"Aldo doesn't have any more copies in stock," I said. "He could probably get me a copy." (Well, there was a *chance* he could get me a copy.) "I just felt like reading it right away."

"Which one is it?" Harold asked suspiciously. "Is it worth anything?" Isn't it just like a collector to be always thinking about monetary value?

"Oh, no," I said. ("Not yet," I added mentally.) "It's just *Larry the Lizard*. I could give you double the cover price. It's not like it's old or anything."

Silence from Harold. Should I offer him more money? No, that would make him suspicious. I should play it cool.

"It's no big deal," I said. "Forget it. I

just thought you might want to do a friend a favor, that's all."

"I would," Harold said quickly. "I would. All right, I'll do it." He gulped.

"Great!" I said. "Meet me in the park in fifteen minutes—and bring the comic!" I hung up before he could change his mind.

RETURNED FROM THE FUTURE

"Oh boy, oh boy, oh boy," I thought as I jogged to the park. "I'm gonna be rich, rich, rich!"

I jumped up and down, spun around, and jogged backward. "Ho ho! Rich Ron Rooney. It's my lucky day!"

I was getting a little short of breath, so I slowed down. "Harold will never suspect," I thought. "Even when he sees how valuable *Larry the Lizard* becomes, he'll never suspect that I saw a page from a *Backstreet's* of the future!"

After a few more steps, I thought, "It serves him right anyway for not reading

his comics. He doesn't *deserve* to have such a special one!"

I got to the park. "And anyway," I said to myself, "it's a dog-eat-dog world. Every man for himself."

Somehow I didn't feel so excited anymore. I sat on a bench under an apple tree. Some sweet-smelling petals floated down past my face. I watched them drift to the ground.

They landed next to a crumpled-up juice cup and a paper wrapper with mustard stains on it.

Littering really burns me up. There was a garbage can about five feet away, for cripes sake!

I picked up the garbage and threw it in the can. Some people are incredibly selfish!

I stopped in my tracks. I stood still. I

felt a hot flush spreading up to the tops of my ears.

Wasn't what I was going to do to Harold *beyond* incredibly selfish? Darn. My conscience had caught up with me again. Now I would have to forget the whole thing. Unless...*hmmm*...maybe I could make a deal with Harold. Say, sell him my secret information for a share of the comic...or something.

Speaking of Harold, shouldn't he be here by now? I looked around the park.

And then I saw him. Not Harold. The man from the future!

THE END OF THE UNIVERSE!

The man from the future bought a hot dog and a bottle of orange soda.

I wondered what hot dogs would be like in 2027. They would probably be made out of soybeans. No wonder he was having one of ours.

He squirted it with a lot of mustard, took a handful of napkins, and sat down on one of the benches.

I looked carefully at his black-and-

white shoes with the pointy toes. Were they time-travel shoes? I couldn't tell.

I wondered if he was wearing the business suit of the future. I tried to picture Mr. Fishbone in a shiny purple suit. I guessed he would look a lot like this guy.

I couldn't take my eyes off him. I hoped he would do something weird.

He unscrewed the cap of his orange soda, took a swallow, and screwed the top back on. Every time he took a swallow, he screwed the top back on.

That's just the queer kind of thing that Harold Fishbone does. The man glanced at his watch. An awful thought popped into my head. Maybe he knows that Harold and I are meeting here today— and that Harold is bringing the comic! Maybe he knows when Harold will be

coming! And he knows he has time to eat his hot dog, and then he'll just walk up and grab the comic from me and Harold, and zap himself back to the future!

Nah! How could he know all that? Then an even more awful thought came to

me. I felt clammy all over. There was only one way he could know all that. He could know all that if he *was* Harold Fishbone! THE GROWN-UP HAROLD FISHBONE, RETURNED TO THE PAST! TRYING TO CHEAT ME OUT OF MY SHARE!

Of course! That must be it. It was the only possible explanation. No wonder he kept reminding me of Mr. Fishbone! He *was* Mr. Fishbone. Mr. *Harold* Fishbone!

So Harold was going to be bald. Just like his father. I gasped and jumped to my feet! I had just realized something. Didn't he know what would happen if he met himself in a different time?!

Of course not. He didn't know because he didn't read his own comics! And if that didn't prove that he was Harold Fishbone, I didn't know what would!

But *I* know what happens if you meet yourself in another time period. And I was scared.

Because what anyone who has read *Spasm* knows is this: When a person meets himself in another time period, the universe IMPLODES!

ARE YOU OR ARE YOU NOT
HAROLD FISHBONE?

The Harold Fishbone from the future took his last bite of hot dog. He wiped his mouth and his hands, and threw his napkin in the trash. Then he went back to the stand and bought a Three Musketeers bar.

That's when I saw young Harold enter the park from the other side. I ran over to him. And keeping my body between the two Harolds, I covered young Harold's

eyes with my arm and tried to turn him around.

"Don't look!" I whispered. "Turn back! Turn back!" Harold kicked and struggled. *"Ouch! Ouch!"* He was tougher than I had expected.

"Help!" he yelled.

"Keep quiet, you fool!" I tripped over his feet and fell down on top of him. He pounded me with his fists.

"HELP! HELP!" he yelled. Somebody big and strong picked me up by the belt. It was the Harold from the future!

Young Harold got to his feet. "Don't look at each other!" I yelled. Naturally, they looked at each other. "EEEAARGH!" I screamed, and hit the dirt, covering my head with both hands.

Nothing happened. The universe did

not implode. I peeked out. Young Harold was picking up his comic, *Larry the Lizard*, number one. It was all scrunched up, and the cover was torn.

"Hey, that's *my* comic!" the Harold from the future said.

"No, it's not! It's ours!" I yelled, jumping up and standing right in front of young Harold with my arms stretched out.

Young Harold kicked me in the back of the leg. I couldn't really blame him, but I wished he wore sneakers like everyone else.

"No, no," said the man, "I know it's yours. I mean, I wrote it!"

I was still suspicious. "Don't let him have it," I said to young Harold.

"What's the matter with you anyway?" young Harold asked. "Look what you did to my comic! I suppose you don't want to buy it now!"

"Were you fighting over my comic?" asked the Harold from the future. He looked sort of pleased.

Everyone was totally confused. Including me. I just wanted to know one thing. "Why didn't the universe implode?!" I asked. The two Harolds looked at me.

"Why should it?" they both said.

I took a deep breath. I stepped back. I looked at the two of them together.

Up close, they didn't look quite so much alike. "Answer me one question," I said, pointing at the man. "Are you or are you not Harold Fishbone?"

"He's off his rocker," young Harold said. He meant me.

"I am not Harold Fishbone," said the man.

"*I'm* Harold Fishbone!" Harold yelled.

"How do you do?" the man said to Harold, shaking his hand. "I'm Bob Elbo, Jr."

"WOW!" I yelled. "*The* Bob Elbo, Jr.? The creator and artist of *Larry the Lizard*?!"

"The same," he said. And he bowed to me.

LARRY THE LIZARD EXPOSED

Harold looked at his comic and at Bob Elbo, Jr. "You mean you wrote this?" he said, holding it up.

Bob Elbo, Jr., smiled and nodded, then reached for the comic.

"Not so fast," I thought to myself. He might be one of the greatest living cartoonists, but I still didn't want him getting his hands on our comic. I grabbed it out of Harold's hand and hid it behind my back.

Then Harold jumped on me, and we were both in the dirt again.

"Hey, hey!" yelled Bob Elbo, Jr.

"What's the big deal about that comic? I'll give you each a new copy. I've got a whole box of them in the car."

My mouth fell open. Then my eyes narrowed. "I thought there were only ten copies left in the world," I said suspiciously. What was going on here?

"WHAT?" yelled Harold. "WHAT! YOU DIRTY RAT! YOU SAID IT WASN'T WORTH ANYTHING!" He took a swing at me.

I put my hands over my head and tried to roll out of the way. "Harold!" I was saying. "Listen to me. I can explain!"

Bob Elbo, Jr., pulled us apart again. He was making sputtering, gasping sorts of noises. "*Mmmph, humph, humph!*" He was laughing!

I took the opportunity to say to Harold, "I wasn't going through with it,

Harold! I realized it was wrong. I was going to tell you all about it!"

"HAH!" said Harold. Mr. Elbo finally stopped laughing.

"I don't know what I'm laughing about," he said. "What a jerk! But who would have thought..."

Harold and I didn't have the slightest idea what he was talking about.

We waited. "I owe you guys an apology," he said. "Let me explain. *Larry the Lizard* is my first comic. But that doesn't mean I haven't been trying to sell comics for a long time. Nobody wanted my stuff. They said it wasn't 'mass-market' enough. They wanted more blood and guts.

"So when I finally got published, I wanted to show everybody. I wanted to be incredibly successful and sell a million copies!

"But they were right. *Larry the Lizard* will never be really successful."

"Hey!" I said. "It *is* successful! It's a great comic! And it's in the space probe—on its way to another galaxy!"

"Really? No kidding? The space probe has my comic in it?"

"Yeah, and I predict it's going to be one of the greatest comics of all time! But you know that already."

"Aaah," said Mr. Elbo. "That's what I have to explain. I guess you found the paper I left in the Invisible Planet?" He looked at us questioningly.

I nodded. Harold looked out of it. "Well, that paper wasn't real," he went on. "It was just a publicity stunt. Just a stupid trick."

"What paper?" asked Harold.

I was dumbfounded. "You mean it

wasn't really from the future? And *you're* not from the future? And *those* aren't time-travel shoes?"

"No, I'm sorry. I'm not from the future."

I was incredibly disappointed.

"What paper?" said Harold.

"I'm sorry," Mr. Elbo said again. He looked at the ground. "Uh, let me get you guys some comics." And he rushed off to where he had parked his car.

"WHAT PAPER?" Harold screamed. So I had to show him the fake page from the *Backstreet's* of Summer, 2027.

BETTER THAN MINT!

Harold was mad all over again.

"I was going to tell you, Harold," I said. "I really was! I'm sorry I ever tried to fool you in the first place."

Harold glared at me over the tops of his glasses. "You're all covered with dirt," he said.

"So are you," I said. And we both started laughing. Harold laughed so hard he got the hiccups.

"And you really thought that guy was me from the future?! *Hyuck, hyuck!*"

I thought he was overdoing it a little bit. "Cool it," I said. "Here comes Mr. Elbo."

Bob Elbo, Jr., gave us each about thirty comics—signed copies of *Larry the Lizard* with our names on them and funny drawings of us (the guy was good) and lots of other cool comics.

"WOW!" said Harold, holding his signed copy of *Larry the Lizard* carefully. "This is *better* than mint! I'm glad my old number one got wrecked because this one is better—and now I can *read* my old one!"

"Hey, Harold, you can come over to my house and read all the comics you want," I said.

"I can?" He looked really happy. "That would be awesome!" I asked him where I could get some of those cool suitcases.

"I send away for them," he said. "You can borrow my catalog."

"Good," I said. "Because I'm saving this comic forever!...Who knows, it might be worth a million dollars someday!"

We looked at Bob Elbo, Jr., and he winked at us. Then he said, "Want to walk over to the Invisible Planet? I was thinking of asking if they wanted to sponsor some cartooning classes. You know, materials, lettering, inking—that kind of thing. Do you think that's a good idea?"

I was speechless. I think I heard Harold say something like, "Sure, me and Ron would come."

I was already thinking about going to cartooning class and showing Bob Elbo,

Jr., my drawings. I was thinking about showing him my new drawing table with the clip-on full-spectrum light. I was thinking about Ron Rooney, future famous cartoonist!

Mr. Elbo opened the door to the Invisible Planet. *BONGGgggggg...*

Don't miss the next Ron Rooney adventure, coming in spring 1997

Space Mall

"OOF! HEY!"

Everybody was pushing me from behind.

I would have fallen right through the doorway. Except it was covered with a sheet of hard plastic or something.

Which was a good thing.

Because I could see through it. And what I saw was THE WHOLE TOWN BELOW ME! About a thousand feet down.

As I watched, it quickly grew smaller and smaller until it disappeared behind some swirling white clouds.

And then I could see the curve of a blue-and-white globe surrounded by the blackness of outer space.

And then the globe shrunk away to nothing. Nothing but star-studded blackness.

ABOUT THE AUTHORS

Jon Buller and Susan Schade get the ideas for their stories from a large rock in their backyard, which broadcasts messages directly to the screen of their computer. They are married and live in Lyme, Connecticut, with their large collection of plastic action figures.